How to Receive from God

HOW TO RECEIVE FROM GOD

MARK AMOATENG, M.D.

How to Receive from God
by Mark Amoateng, M.D.

Cover Design by Atinad Designs.

© Copyright 2015

SAINT PAUL PRESS, DALLAS, TEXAS

First Printing, 2015

All rights reserved. No part of this publication may be reproduced, stored in a retrieval system, or transmitted in any form or by any means, electronic, mechanical, photocopying, recording, or otherwise, without the prior permission of the copyright owner, except for brief quotations included in a review of the book.

ISBN-10: 0996324119
ISBN-13: 978-0-9963241-1-3

Printed in the U.S.A.

This book is dedicated to the
Lord Jesus Christ.
There is no one like Him.

Contents

Foreword 9
Introduction 11

Chapter 1 15
    Receiving not Achieving

Chapter 2 27
    God is a Giver

Chapter 3 37
    The Universe of God: the Spiritual Realm
    and the Physical Realm

Chapter 4 49
    How to Receive

Chapter 5 63
    Thoughts and Emotions

Chapter 6 71
    The Hindrances to Receiving

Foreword

Ever since I first met Dr. Mark Amoateng, I was impressed on how well he could express himself to the point of convincing others to receive at least a portion of what he has found in God. It is with this in mind that I forward this to you. Anyone who is interested in finding their purpose in God should read this book from beginning to end. It is filled with the Word of God showing a clear path on how to receive from God. Dr. Mark makes it clear that it is not just he who hears the Word, but he who receives the Word that causes him to become ingrafted so that he can receive from God. I highly recommend this book to anyone who wants to be grounded in the Word and established in the ministry. Everyone should be excited about receiving a clear simple answer on how to receive from God. What greater blessing is there?

Sincerely,

God's General
C.S. Upthegrove

Introduction

Matthew 7:8:
"For everyone who asks receives; he who seeks finds; and to him who knocks, the door will be opened" (NIV).

Everyone who asks receives. That is the law of God. I thought God would say everyone who asks I will give. The giving has already been done, so there is no need to echo that. God is a giver. He gives and gives till it sometimes overflows. God will always give you as much as you can handle. But everything God gives must be received. It is a law.

God has ways of doing things. His ways of operation form the laws of His Kingdom. There are laws in the Kingdom of God.

One of His laws is the *law of receiving*.

Whatever you ask you must first receive before you can have. Most people wait to have without receiving and so they never have. What do you have that you did not receive? In 1 Corinthians 4:7, we read: *"For who maketh thee to differ from another? And what hast thou that thou didst not receive? Now if thou didst receive it, why dost thou glory, as if thou hadst not received it?"*

I John 3:22 states: *"And whatsoever we ask, we receive of him, because we keep his commandments, and do those things that are pleasing in his sight."*

Whatever you ask you must receive.

Maybe you prayed for what you desire, and after several years there are no signs of you seeing your desire fulfilled. I am sure you started asking questions like: Did God hear me? Is God angry with me? Well, I am sure God's heard you for a long time, because He is not hard of hearing, and He has given whatever you asked of Him, because His hands are not short (Isaiah 59). What if you believe that everything you ever ask from God He has already provided and He is just waiting on you to receive it? Now the question is, how do you receive it?

There is a way to receive. And we have to learn to receive. Many have learned to ask, but have not learned to receive.

This is what you will discover in this book: *How to receive from God: the mechanism.*

In this book we shall explore the first principles of how to receive from God, so that your prayers are answered one hundred percent of the time.

As you discover these principles, believe them, adhere to them, practice them and you will live in continual flow of having whatever you ask of God.

As you apply this law of God strictly, diligently, and consistently, success shall be your story. You will become a wonder in your world.

Light from Heaven is coming your way to shatter every darkness in your life. A stream of testimonies and answered prayers await you after this adventure.

Chapter One
Receiving not Achieving

There are laws and principles that govern every system, every nation, and every kingdom. The universe itself is governed by laws. For example, there is the law of gravity that attracts people to the centre of the earth whether they know it or not. Laws function whether you believe in them or not. Those who know, understand, and apply the laws are those who benefit the most or reign in any particular system.

The kingdom of God is governed by laws, principles, and rudiments. And those who bring themselves in harmony with these laws will always be victorious and reign as kings and masters in life. Laws are meant to be observed or applied to see results.

"That they might observe his statutes, and keep his laws. Praise ye the LORD" (Psalm 105:45).

The man who is blessed by God is the man who fears Him. And the man who fears God is the man who delights in and applies His laws.

"Praise ye the LORD. Blessed is the man that feareth the LORD, that delighteth greatly in his commandments" (Psalm 112:1).

God and His laws are impartial. Anyone who applies His laws will get the same results. God plays no favourites! Nothing could be plainer than this. It makes no difference who you are or where you are from, if you desire God and apply His laws, the door is open always. This is the truth of God.

"Then Peter opened his mouth, and said, Of a truth I perceive that God is no respecter of persons" (Acts 10:34).

The world system, too, has its laws, principles, and traditions.

"Beware lest any man spoil you through philosophy and vain deceit, after the tradition of men, after the rudiments of the world, and not after Christ" (Colossians 2:8).

The reason the sons and daughters of the Creator and Ruler of the universe live small and mediocre lives is not because God is not powerful, neither is it because God is not loving, or the enemy of God's children, the devil, is too powerful. No. The only reason is the lack of knowledge of God and His laws.

"My people are destroyed for lack of knowledge: because thou hast rejected knowledge, I will also reject thee, that thou shalt be no priest to me: seeing thou hast forgotten the law of thy God, I will also forget thy children" (Hosea 4:6).

"Therefore my people are gone into captivity, because they have no knowledge: and their honourable men are famished, and their multitude dried up with thirst" (Isaiah 5:13).

"And by knowledge shall the chambers be filled with all precious and pleasant riches. A wise man is strong; yea, a man of knowledge increaseth strength" (Proverbs 24:4-5).

My people are destroyed for lack of knowledge, God laments for His people. Men are in bondage for the lack of knowledge. Honorable men and women with great destinies are being stripped of their dignity day in and day out. But a man of knowledge will break forth suddenly into his destiny, because every strength you need for your glorification is a function of your knowledge.

Knowledge is the greatest asset in every endeavour of life. Every outstanding transformation can be traced to a revealed knowledge. When you properly trade with revealed knowledge, it brings you your desired end. Knowledge is light, and it is the Word of God which releases that light. *"The entrance of thy words giveth light; it giveth understanding unto the simple"* (Psalm 119:130). The entrance of God's Word gives light. When you encounter God's Word on any issue, darkness can no longer hold you in that area. And the light shines in darkness and the darkness comprehends it not. God's Word says, *"Arise and shine for thy light is come."* Nobody can shine until light comes and the light cannot come until the Word enters.

You cannot win in God's Kingdom whilst applying the laws of the world or the world's way of doing things. To win in God's system you must apply His laws. And most of the time the laws of the Kingdom are antagonistic, or they disagree with the laws of the world.

For example, in the world we gain by hoarding or saving, but in God's Kingdom you gain by giving: *"The liberal soul shall be made fat: and he that watereth shall be watered also himself"* (Proverbs 11:25). In the Kingdom of God we increase by sharing, and reap by sowing; we are lifted by lifting others. That means becoming a servant. But the world system tells you, you diminish by sharing, you are demoted when you serve, and you can even reap without sowing. And the system of the world considers the principles of God's Kingdom as foolishness. But even 'the foolishness of God is wiser than man's wisdom.'

In the Kingdom is *the principle called receiving*. The Scriptures say, *"For who maketh thee to differ from another? and what hast thou that thou didst not receive? now if thou didst receive it, why dost thou glory, as if thou hadst not received it?"* (I Corinthians 4:7). The above scriptural verse is asking, what do you have that you did not receive? Whatever you have ever had in the Kingdom was received not achieved, and whatever you will ever have in the Kingdom must be received and not achieved. The reason you just have to receive is all because the work has been done. Jesus has already achieved for you.

Understanding that all you have to do is to receive takes away boasting, glorying, and priding in self. *"Now if thou didst receive it, why dost thou glory, as if thou hadst not received it?"* (I Corinthians 4:7b).

Knowing that you can only receive from a loving God makes you dependent on that loving God who lives in you by His Holy Spirit. And this is what God wants. The aim of God is to produce in you dependence on Him and not performance. The whole Bible is about receiving and not achieving. From the beginning that has been the principle in operation. Adam received a beautiful estate called the

Garden of Eden. He received a lot of different pets in his home. He had no swimming pool but had four rivers in his estate. He received a wife called Eve. They were all gifts God bestowed. He didn't have to achieve them or work for them. All he had to do was to receive.

In Heaven, too, God will lavish on us great gifts, happiness, and a lot of pleasures—even more than He gave Adam. If you don't learn to receive here on earth you might even try to work and achieve your own happiness and pleasures in Heaven. But the Bible says those happiness and pleasures are already prepared and just waiting for you. *"Thou wilt shew me the path of life: in thy presence is fulness of joy; at thy right hand there are pleasures for evermore"* (Psalm 16:11). At the right hand of God are pleasures forever more. We will have to just receive. Glory be to God. We will not have to work for them or achieve them. Your knowledge to receive and capacity to receive is paramount in this Kingdom of God.

The culture and rudiments of the world system tell you otherwise. It tells you, you have to achieve first before you receive. For example, you work before you get your wages, your salary, or your bonuses; and people must earn their love. But it is not so with the Kingdom of God.

Right from salvation and throughout your walk in the Kingdom of God it is all about receiving. *"He came unto his own, and his own received him not. But as many as received him, to them gave he power to become the sons of God, even to them that believe on his name"* (John 1:11-12). It is those who receive Him, not those who achieve Him. You receive Christ because Christ is a gift. *"As ye have therefore received Christ Jesus the Lord, so walk ye in him"*

(Colossians 2:8). Ye therefore received Christ.

"But to him that worketh not, but believeth on him that justifieth the ungodly, his faith is counted for righteousness" (Romans 4:5). Salvation does not come from working or doing some good or stacking up enough good deeds to earn God's favour. It is the finished work of Christ that brings salvation and secures us eternally and upon which work all things are given us. It was Christ who worked for you. You could not work to save yourself, and you did not know what work to do in the first place. The works were finished from the foundations of the world. And Jesus who worked the works was crucified from the foundations of the world. And Jesus said my Father works and I work. So actually the Father Himself worked the works for you. Hallelujah! Isn't God good? He is saying to you, 'I have worked; just come and receive the dividends of my work.'

"Beloved, when I gave all diligence to write unto you of the common salvation, it was needful for me to write unto you, and exhort you that ye should earnestly contend for the faith which was once delivered unto the saints" (Jude 1:3). The writer is talking about salvation, and he said a kind of faith was delivered. What was delivered must only be received—not worked for or achieved. Potentially, Jesus has saved all men. He purchased redemption and gave His life for all men. The Bible says the grace of God which brings salvation has appeared to *all* men.

The last time I checked all meant all, including everybody, excluding nobody; whether male or female, black or white, red or indigo, young or old, rich or poor. The grace of God that brings salvation has appeared to all men. Nobody needs to live the next moment of their lives without God's salvation. Nobody must die unsaved because the grace that brings salvation has appeared. It has been revealed.

That salvation includes well-being, prosperity, health, preservation, and deliverance. You must not live in poverty and penury because that grace, which brings prosperity, has appeared. You must not live in bondage and oppression, because that grace which brings deliverance has appeared. You must not be held down by sickness and disease because that grace which brings salvation has appeared. You must not go through that emotional trauma in your relationship and marriage, because that grace which brings soundness and peace of mind has appeared.

That Grace is a person, even Jesus Christ, and He brings you healing and health, prosperity and wholeness. And Grace is calling out to everyone and everybody. It is saying: I have justification, I have eternal security, I have healing and prosperity. And yet not everyone is saved, justified, healed, and prosperous. The reason is simple. Not everyone has received. Very few have received that Grace. Most people are still trying to achieve all of these. The Scripture said, they which receive abundance of grace ... shall reign in life.

"For if by one man's offence death reigned by one; much more they which receive abundance of grace and of the gift of righteousness shall reign in life by one, Jesus Christ" (Romans 5:17). There is grace to make you reign. Have you received it? That grace is exhaustless, limitless. The Scripture says that grace is in abundance. You can take abundance and still have abundance remaining. There is abundance for

everybody. He came that you might have life and have it more abundantly. Glory be to God.

When a child is born, he does not have to buy diapers, he does not have to go and work for his food. He does not have to work for love and care. He does not work for his identity. He just simply must receive them. The baby would not have to impress anyone. Even so in the Kingdom of God. Till you receive the Kingdom as a little child you will run from failure to failure and defeat to defeat. *"And said, Verily I say unto you, Except ye be converted, and become as little children, ye shall not enter into the kingdom of heaven"* (Matthew 18:3).

You must convert to have the little child's mentality who just receives and does not try to achieve. Wouldn't it be strange if your day old baby told you, 'Mummy, what can I do for you so you give me diapers?' I am sure you will be shocked to your very core. So then why do you do that to your heavenly Father? *"If ye then, being evil, know how to give good gifts unto your children, how much more shall your Father which is in heaven give good things to them that ask him?"* (Matthew 7:11). So just learn to receive as a little child.

Your identity and nature as a believer were not achieved but received. Romans 5:17b says, *"...and the gift of righteousness."* This righteousness is now your nature. You did not work for that nature and identity. You only received it. *"For he hath made him to be sin for us, who knew no sin; that we might be made the righteousness of God in him"* (2 Corinthians 5:21). And once you receive your identity you now work from it. In the Kingdom of God, unlike in the world, you don't work for your identity, but you work from your identity. You may ask what's the difference? Or you might say it is just a play on words. No, it is not. It means you are not going to do righteous acts to be righteous [working for your identity], but because you have been declared righteous and have the nature of righteousness you do righteous acts [working from your identity].

When you work for or achieve your identity or things in the Kingdom, then you can boast or glory in your works. But God wants no one to boast before Him. *"That no flesh shall glory in His presence"* (1 Corinthians 1:29). Such glorying originates in the fleshly nature. The fleshly man wants to work and achieve so that he can boast. That nature wants to try hard to obtain his salvation. That nature wants to try hard to obtain his healing. That nature wants to try hard to obtain his forgiveness or deliverance so he can go about telling everyone how hardworking he is and how much better he is than everybody else.

"For the wages of sin is death; but the gift of God is eternal life through Jesus Christ our Lord" (Romans 6:23). This Scripture reveals two systems: The Wage system of the world and the Gift system of God. The Wage system, which is the world system, deals with wages. That is achieving. You work and you earn. But God's system deals with you receiving gifts then working with the gifts. It is God giving gifts to His children, and His children receiving them.

When the world system gives you a gift, it is to motivate you to work and most of the time is conditional. But God's gifts are not conditional and they are not to motivate you. They are expressions of His love. *"For the gifts and calling of God are without repentance"* (Romans 11:29). His gifts are irrevocable. In the world system you have to qualify for the gifts, but with God the gift qualifies you.

The anointing or grace of God you received was freely given. It is not how hard you prayed, although you might have prayed hard; but somebody prayed more than you did and yet does not have what you have. It is not how 'hard' you fasted although you might have fasted 'hard'; but somebody fasted more than you and still cannot do what you can do. Who then makes you to differ from one another? The answer is still in 2 Corinthians 4:7: 'what do you have that you did not receive.' *"But we have this treasure in earthen vessels, that the excellency of the power may be of God, and not of us."*

Now those who think they worked for the anointing or the Grace of God now want others to work or pay them before they benefit from that anointing. But Scripture says freely you have received, so you too freely give. That does not mean don't get blessed from the gifting of God. The gift will bless you and make room for you. Hallelujah. *"A man's gift maketh room for him, and bringeth him before great men"* (Proverbs 18:16).

"Who goeth a warfare any time at his own charges? who planteth a vineyard, and eateth not of the fruit thereof? or who feedeth a flock, and eateth not of the milk of the flock? Say I these things as a man? or saith not the law the same also? For it is written in the law of Moses, Thou shalt not muzzle the mouth of the ox that treadeth out the corn. Doth God take care for oxen?" (I Corinthians 9:7-9).

A lot of people are frustrated because they have been trying to achieve or work for some great anointing or healing or deliverance, or for happiness and peace and only God knows how long it has eluded them. It has left them depressed and miserable. Such people have come to the conclusion that the Gospel does not work, prayers are hardly answered, or even that God is wicked. They tell you how much they fasted and prayed, and yet, did not receive their healing. They tell you I gave this amount of money to God and am still broke. If only such people knew that it is about receiving and not achieving, they will seek for the means to receive.

This book is about showing you how to receive. Frustration among believers is a result of trying to go against the laws of the Kingdom. To the one who hath (the one who has learned to receive), more shall be given, the Scriptures say. It sounds very unfair, but that is the law. Just stick with His laws, and you are bound to excel and live abundantly.

Chapter Two

God is a Giver

The reason why in God's Kingdom you receive and not achieve is simply because God is a giver and He has already provided for all of humanity enough of everything to last us for eternity.

"He that spared not his own Son, but delivered him up for us all, how shall he not with him also freely give us all things?" (Romans 8.32).

Paul makes a great argument here. If God gave His only Son for us, how will He not have added freely all other things? God gave His best and His all in Jesus. When God gave us Jesus He gave everything else to us. In John 3:16, we read, *"For God so loved the world, that he gave his only begotten Son, that whosoever believeth in him should not perish, but have everlasting life."* God gave us Jesus.

God never said I am giving you healing, resurrection, deliverance, or money. The Scripture only says 'for God so loved us that he gave his only begotten son.' But beloved, here is the great news of the Gospel: when God gave you

Jesus He gave you everything else, because all things are in Him. In Him all things consist. *"For by him were all things created, that are in heaven, and that are in earth, visible and invisible, whether they be thrones, or dominions, or principalities, or powers: all things were created by him, and for him: And he is before all things, and by him all things consist"* (Colossians 1:16-17).

God is a giver. We are told in James 1:17: *"Every good gift and every perfect gift is from above, and cometh down from the Father of lights, with whom is no variableness, neither shadow of turning."*

"John answered and said, A man can receive nothing, except it be given him from heaven" (John 3:27). A man can receive nothing unless it is given to him from above. Everything is given by God. He is the great Giver.

"Now we have received, not the spirit of the world, but the spirit which is of God; that we might know the things that are freely given to us of God. Which things also we speak, not in the words which man's wisdom teacheth, but which the Holy Ghost teacheth; comparing spiritual things with spiritual" (1 Corinthians 2:12-13).

What God has given was given freely without cost to you. You don't have to buy it with money, you don't have to work for it, but rather just come and receive it. *"Ho, every one that thirsteth, come ye to the waters, and he that hath no money; come ye, buy, and eat; yea, come, buy wine and milk without money and without price. Wherefore do ye spend money for that which is not bread? and your labour for that which satisfieth not? hearken diligently unto me, and eat ye that which is good, and let your soul delight itself in fatness"* (Isaiah 55:1-2).

God is calling you and everyone to come, and freely receive.

One of the purposes of the Holy Spirit is to search the depth of God and find out what has been freely given and make it known to you. The Holy Spirit is like a professor who comes to show you what he knows through his search and researches. For the depths of God are great and deep and past finding out. *"O the depth of the riches both of the wisdom and knowledge of God! how unsearchable are his judgments, and his ways past finding out!"* (Romans 11:33).

The Spirit accesses them for you and delivers them to you. And all you've got to do is to receive. That is why you have to make the Holy Spirit your greatest and best friend in life. The Holy Spirit reminds you or brings to your remembrance all things God has given in Jesus. *"But the Comforter, which is the Holy Ghost, whom the Father will send in my name, he shall teach you all things, and bring all things to your remembrance, whatsoever I have said unto you"* (John 14:26).

God is a great God of love. Actually, He is the embodiment of love. He does not only give love; He is love. Because of His nature there is nothing that He can give that He has not already given. He is a God who lavishes His children with exceeding grace and glory.

And again He is the all powerful God. His power is inexpressible, indescribable, and ineffable. I call him the TOO MUCH GOD. His power is boundless, all encompassing, and eternal. It is impossible to ask, desire, or request anything too great or too much for God to do or give to you. He said 'I am God. Is there anything too hard or difficult for me.' God is in the business of giving, and He is always looking for every avenue to dispense. He does not want to dispense or give little.

People are afraid to ask from God because they either feel God cannot do it or will not do it. And others think if they ask moderately or little it means they are humble or very spiritual. No and a big NO. Actually, the more powerful and mighty the desires of a person's heart, the closer the person is to God. The greater your request, vision, and desire, the more pleased God is with you. God wants children who will ask big things from Him. Dare to believe God. Ask Him that which beats the imagination and achievements of men. Don't limit Him as the Israelites did. The psalmist tells us, *"and they limited the Holy one of Israel"* (Psalm 78:41b).

The Bible says *"open thy mouth wide and I will fill it"* (Psalm 81:10). How wide can you open it? How wide will you open it? God has given you the ocean, why come with a cup to fetch? Why come with a drinking straw to sip? Ask because you have a big God as your father. God is bigger, greater, stronger, and more loving than people imagine Him to be. When you just get a glimpse of the vastness of God's throne and glory, you will throw off the shackles and chains of small thinking and small asking. The great Father longs for His children to have the proudest cravings, the largest expectations for He has infinity of blessings, which it is His happiness to bestow. The more you desire from Him, the more you shall have. Don't bind God down and restrict His great power from operating in your life with your little, puny, mortal thoughts.

God wants us to enlarge our thoughts and spread our wings. *"Enlarge the place of thy tent, and let them stretch forth the curtains of thine habitations: spare not, lengthen thy cords, and strengthen thy stakes"* (Isaiah 54:2). Enlarge your tents, enlarge your coast, enlarge your horizon and ask big things from a big God.

It is imposssible to ask or desire anything too great so long as it is for His glory. It is impossible to believe too much. It is impossible to desire too much. It is impossible to hope or ask for too much. God has given the best and the greatest already. He gave His only beloved Son. *"Whereby are given unto us exceeding great and precious promises: that by these ye might be partakers of the divine nature, having escaped the corruption that is in the world through lust"* (2 Peter1:4). We have superlative promises. Hallelujah. When you ask or think little, God does not lose or change. What happens is, you lose and remain impotent and helpless for asking too little. You remain restricted because you hope too little. When you think skimpy, meagre, and little thoughts you are feeding on crumbs, which is for dogs and not for children of the great God of the universe.

When you believe God for the impossible, you have access to the limitless ability of God. *"Jesus said unto him, If thou canst believe, all things are possible to him that believeth"* (Mark 9:23). The reason all things are possible to him who believes is because, he has the ability of God at his disposal, for *"with God all things are possible"* (Matthew 19:26). The person who believes is with God in the same dimension. The one who believes lives on the same street with God called POSSIBILITY STREET. Glory be to God!

Responsibility

Now you may say, if we just tell people to receive and not achieve or do nothing, it will produce lazy believers. No, it won't. It is the traditions and the rudiments of men which has programmed humanity that way, so when you talk about the graciousness of God they think it is too good to be true. They compare God, the heavenly Father with their earthly fathers. They only received gifts from their earthly parents only after working for something. For example, when you come up first in your class or at graduation, or special occasions like wedding and the like.

To receive and not to achieve is what is called Grace. It is God's unmerited favor towards men. It is His goodwill towards His race. *"Glory to God in the highest, and on earth peace, good will toward men"* (Luke 2:14). When Jesus was born, God received glory, and goodwill came to men. This was the twofold purpose of Jesus coming, glory to God in the highest, and on earth peace and goodwill towards men. This is what is called grace. Grace is glory to God and goodwill towards men. And this is supposed to be the state and lifestyle of men. Men must live as those receiving goodwill from a loving God. Goodwill is satisfaction, delight, and kindness. God's purpose of bringing Jesus is to give men satisfaction and bestow on them great kindness. True satisfaction and fulfillment can only be found with Jesus. Grace was meant to be lived not debated upon. Grace is a lifestyle. Your life was meant to be gracious.

Now with grace comes responsibility. In biblical numerology the number five symbolises grace, and it also symbolises responsibility. You have five fingers with which you work. In Ephesians 4:11-12, we read, *"And he gave some, apostles; and some, prophets; and some, evangelists; and some, pastors and teachers; For the perfecting of the saints, for the work of the ministry, for the edifying of the body of Christ."* The fivefold ministry is revealed. They work with the saints after perfecting them. So five, too, stands for responsibility.

The responsibility of the believer is twofold. The first responsibility is to Receive. It is the responsibility of the believer to receive what God has already given. If I bring a billion dollar to you as a gift, you have a responsibility to open the door, stretch out your hand and receive the cheque or bags of cash. If I deposit it in the bank you will have to go to the bank or log into your account online or on your mobile app to access the money that has already been given to you. Nobody can receive for you, not even God. God is a good and gentle Father. He is not going about forcing Himself and things on people. He is only announcing to everyone what He out of His freewill has made available to all men.

In the book of John the fifth chapter this type of responsibility is well illustrated. *"Jesus saith unto him, Rise, take up thy bed, and walk. And immediately the man was made whole, and took up his bed, and walked: and on the same day was the sabbath"* (John 5:8-9). Jesus has the healing power, and He is giving it to the man, and He says rise up, take up your bed, and walk. Jesus gave the healing power and the man had to receive. But how did the man receive? He received by responding to the command of Jesus. Rising, taking up his mat, and walking was his responsibility. Jesus will not rise for him. Jesus will not walk for him. His rising and his walking is his responsibility. But the healing power was released by Jesus.

The second type of responsibility comes after receiving. *"Freely you have received, freely give"* (Matthew 10:8). You are not just to receive for your enjoyment. God always provides more than enough, so as you enjoy, you will be giving. You receive abundant life so you can give life. You receive hope so you will give hope to the hopeless. You receive help so you will give help to the helpless. You received a home so you can give home to the homeless. You receive riches so you will be rich and generous towards others. God always 'abundantly satisfies us with the fatness of his house' (Psalm 36:8). You receive abundant grace so you can be gracious to others. You receive abundant prosperity so you can make others rich. Glory be to God.

God expects us to be givers like Himself. He is proud when He sees you giving like He does. But you cannot give what you don't have. (Acts 3:6). Such as I have give I thee.

And you cannot have without receiving. The plan of God is to make you a giver so that together with Him you become partners in giving. But till we learn to receive, we will not have, and if we don't have we can't give. So God starts a process of giving, then we receive to have, then we give, so that by this process the influence of the Kingdom spreads to the ends of the world. And the kingdoms of this world becomes the kingdom of our God and of His Christ. Hallelujah.

There are those who cannot give forgiveness because they never learned to receive it themselves. They can't give love because they never learned to receive love. You can't give what you do not have, and you can't have without receiving.

The earth gives food to the whole earth, but it, of a necessity, must receive before it gives. The day it refuses to receive or fails to receive it will lie barren. In the same vein a woman in her reproductive years all other things being equal, *'ceteris paribus,'* has the ability to bring forth, but she must receive the seed from a man first. The believer has the ability to live an abundant life and reign victoriously in life, but he will have to learn to receive first.

There are those who want to do something for God so they can earn something from Him. The best you can do for God is in the book of Romans 12:1, which states in the Message Bible:

"....embracing what God does for you is the best thing you can do for him."

Chapter Three

The Universe of God: the Spiritual Realm and the Physical Realm

My goal is to show you from first principles how you can receive from God any time you pray. And a clear understanding of the spiritual realm and the physical realm is part of the first principles to receive.

"Therefore I say unto you, What things soever ye desire, when ye pray, believe that ye receive them, and ye shall have them" (Mark 11:24).

The verse above is one of the most blessed verses in the Bible. *'What things so ever'* — that is like a blank cheque right there — Divinity will deliver to you according to your desire. What will be delivered to the righteous is determined by his desire. *"The fear of the wicked, it shall come upon him: but the desire of the righteous shall be granted"* (Proverbs 10:24). Once you desire and pray you simply believe you have received and then you shall have. Too good to be true. Man's problem is that God is too good.

People ask, can God give me what I desire? Can it really be that simple? Actually God is not going to give you, He has already given you what you desire. God is all powerful and knows your mind cannot ask Him or desire anything too big that He God cannot provide or that He God has not provided.

God gives us the process of realizing our every desire. He says Desire, Pray, Believe, and Have. Just as simple as that. I call it DPBH. Now you may say, I have been applying this formula ever since and it does not work. The Bible says "let God be true and every man a liar." By two immutable things in which it is impossible for God to lie. God's Word is ever true and He is ever faithful. The integrity of His Word is unquestionable. The problem is a lack of accurate knowledge in the application of His Word. Just hearing the Word or reading the Bible is not the solution. *'You shall know the truth and the truth will make you free'* (John 8:32). The 'know' in this verse is to understand, to be sure, to know as reality and with certainty. It is not just reading or hearing once. It is coming to a perfect understanding of the Word. We should yield to the Holy Spirit's teaching so we may truly know. There is an ancient Arabian proverb which says:

> He who knows not and knows not that he knows not is a fool, avoid him,
> He who knows not and knows that he knows not is simple, teach him,
> He who knows and knows not that he knows is asleep, awake him,
> And he who knows and knows that he knows is wise, follow him.

God gave us a command to prove all things and hold fast to that which is good. But man is going about trying to disprove all things God has said and even the existence of God Himself.

The law of God is that all prayers must be answered. He who seeks finds; everyone who asks receives; he who knocks the door is opened to him. But the unbelieving seek only to disprove what they find, they knock only to reject the invitation to enter in, they ask only to mock what they ought to receive. The proof of desire is pursuit, so prayer now becomes the conduit and channel by which you prove or pursue your desire.

When you desire, you must pray. It is not just a wish. It is a desire. It is that thing which is upon your heart that you want badly. Desire must not be a passive wish. Desire is the soul of prayer. The prayers you pray must be heartfelt and inflamed with red hot desire. Man has a vast capacity for desire. And man's greatest desires are not awakened until they are consciously turned God-ward. The limitedness or limitlessness of a man is determined by his desire. "You are not restricted by us, but you are restricted by your *own* affections" (I Corinthians 6:12, NKJV).

This Scripture indicates that the restriction or resplendence of a man is a product of his affection (desire). The Message Bible says, *"We didn't fence you in. The smallness you feel comes from within you. Your lives aren't small, but you're living them in a small way. I'm speaking as plainly as I can and with great affection. Open up your lives. Live openly and expansively!"* (2 Corinthians 6:12-13, MSG) *"Surely I would speak to the Almighty, and I desire to reason with God"* (Job 13:3).

Desire is the vehicle that drives a man to reason with God. Desire is a gracious gift that makes room for a man and brings him to the realm of greatness and glory. What you do not desire, you cannot demonstrate. The destiny of a man is the description and demonstration of his desires. Your desires determine your declarations, and your declarations determine your destiny. Your delight as a king in the salvation and strength of the Lord is primarily connected to your desires being fulfilled.

"The king shall joy in thy strength, O LORD; and in thy salvation how greatly shall he rejoice! Thou hast given him his heart's desire, and hast not withholden the request of his lips. Selah" (Psalm 21:1-2).

When you pray, the Bible says believe you have received them, then you shall have. Most people after prayer believe they shall receive what they asked for and so they never have. You must receive it in prayer before you can have. Till you receive it in prayer you might wait for eternity and you will never have. Then you will sink into depression and frustration and start blaming God that He did not answer your prayer. But God answered you a long time ago. For the Bible says, *"And it shall come to pass, that before they call, I will answer; and while they are yet speaking, I will hear"* (Isaiah 65:24). You failed to receive what God already gave. Until you learn to receive in prayer you might never have. What do you have that you did not receive? Remember, the Scriptures cannot be broken. You must receive to have.

So now I am sure you are asking yourself, so how do I receive?

To be able to receive you must have a perfect understanding of the dimensions of God's universe.

God created one universe comprising of two dimensions or realms.

These are:
1. The spiritual or unseen or heavenly realm or eternal realm or eternity.
2. The physical or seen or earthly realm or the time realm.

Genesis 1:1 states, *"In the beginning God made the heavens and the earth."* It is not just talking about the earth and the sky. The 'heavens' is referring to the spiritual world that exists parallel to the physical world. *"Now it came to pass in the thirtieth year, in the fourth month, in the fifth day of the month, as I was among the captives by the river of Chebar, that the heavens were opened, and I saw visions of God"* (Ezekiel 1:1). *"Now when all the people were baptized, it came to pass, that Jesus also being baptized, and praying, the heaven was opened"* (Luke 3:21).

The heavens were opened to Ezekiel and Jesus. It is not that the physical sky was opened literally, but that the spiritual realm was opened and they saw the visions of God.

God created a multi-dimensional universe. Because of our materialistic education we assume that the physical realm is all that exists. And if something cannot be scientifically observed, then it is not real. An accurate understanding of the difference between these two dimensions and their relative significance will no doubt enable you to receive what-so-ever things you desire when you pray.

The realm of the spirit is the eternal realm or eternity. There is no space, distance, or time in the spiritual realm. There is no past, present, or future in this realm. Actually the past, present, and future are fused as one. The spiritual realm or eternal is an ever-present now in which the past is never past, and the future is always present. Eternity is not run by watches or calendars. It is run and governed by revelation and faith. Eternity is not some long extension of time. It is just a glorious existence of being. The spiritual realm is the abode of spirits and spiritual activity.

God dwells in eternity. He is not bound by time. So God sees all time equally. There is no succession of moments in His being. God just is. He does not live progressively. He simply just is. So God calls Himself I AM. This is because He lives in an ever-present continuous realm or dimension. He is referred to as the everlasting contemporary. He is the one who was, who is, and who is to come.

Whatever is done in the spiritual realm cannot be lost since there is no passing of time. Every work done or accomplished through the spirit is preserved because it is in the eternal realm. That is why the blood of Jesus Christ is still efficacious today. Hebrews 9:14 says, He offered Himself through the eternal spirit. The blood saved yesterday, it is saving today, and it will save tomorrow, because it was offered through the eternal spirit. Every work done in the spiritual realm cannot fade or be corrupted. It is because of this that the Scriptures can say Jesus was crucified from the foundations of the world. In time, Jesus was crucified about two thousand years ago, but in the spiritual realm that act of the crucifixion of Jesus is boundless. It is always present.

In the spiritual realm the past and present and future are merged into one continuous state. What we know as time does not exist in this realm.

When a man understands this realm and operates from there he can bring the future into now and the past into the present. He can taste of the powers of the ages to come. The future you cannot see in the physical dimension is already a present continuous reality now in the spiritual or unseen realm. And even though God lives in the spiritual realm, He sees into the physical realm and acts in the physical realm or the realm called Time.

So what is the time realm or physical realm or the Seen realm? This realm is simply a venue. It is a location or place where things or events in the spiritual realm can be deposited, dumped, or transported to.

The pieces of events or things assembled together or manufactured in the spiritual realm are deposited or manifested in the venue called Time. Time is the unfolding of moments and events.

What you called past or future actually exists now. With the right eyes you can behold the past, the present, and the future at the same time. The spiritual realm controls the physical realm because the physical was made by the spiritual. Hebrews 11:3, NIV, states, *"By faith we understand that the universe was formed at God's command, so that what is seen was not made out of what was visible."* The above Scripture says the seen was made from the invisible.

The two realms exist side by side simultaneously interacting with each other. The story of Elisha and his servant makes it clearer.

> "*And one of his servants said, None, my lord, O king: but Elisha, the prophet that is in Israel, telleth the king of Israel the words that thou speakest in thy bedchamber.*
>
> "*And he said, Go and spy where he is, that I may send and fetch him. And it was told him, saying, Behold, he is in Dothan.*
>
> "*Therefore sent he thither horses, and chariots, and a great host: and they came by night, and compassed the city about.*
>
> "*And when the servant of the man of God was risen early, and gone forth, behold, an host compassed the city both with horses and chariots. And his servant said unto him, Alas, my master! how shall we do?*
>
> "*And he answered, Fear not: for they that be with us are more than they that be with them.*
>
> "*And Elisha prayed, and said, LORD, I pray thee, open his eyes, that he may see. And the LORD opened the eyes of the young man; and he saw: and, behold, the mountain was full of horses and chariots of fire round about Elisha*" (2 Kings 6:12-17).

Physically they were alone without any help whatsoever. In the spiritual realm which existed right there, there was a host with them. You may be alone in your room as you read this book, but I promise you, if your spiritual eyes should be opened, you will see your guardian angel right with you. Hallelujah. Don't be moved by what you see with your physical eyes only. Be moved by the Word of God. Why? Because the Word of God is Spirit.

"Jesus answered, My kingdom is not of this world: if my kingdom were of this world, then would my servants fight, that I should not be delivered to the Jews: but now is my kingdom not from hence" (John 18:36). Jesus said my Kingdom is not of this world. There is another world or realm which Jesus referred to. It is the spiritual realm. It exists simultaneously with the physical realm. You don't have to travel long distance to be there. You can be there at the speed of a thought.

There is the physical senses with which we relate to the physical realm. The sense of sight, hearing, touch, smell, and taste. And by these senses things are perceived in the physical dimension. There are corresponding senses in the spiritual realm with which to perceive things in the spiritual realm.

The spiritual realm is just as real as the physical. It is even more real than the physical. The physical is referred to as mist or vapour or smoke. *"Whereas ye know not what shall be on the morrow. For what is your life? It is even a vapour that appeareth for a little time, and then vanisheth away"* (James 4:14). *"O remember that my life is wind: mine eye shall no more see good"* (Job 7:7).

"For my days are consumed like smoke, and my bones are burned as an hearth" (Psalm 102:3).

All the above verses prove that this physical world in comparison with the spiritual realm is a mist or vapour or mere smoke. The things of this world are intangible compared to the spiritual. What is real, tangible, and enduring is in the spiritual realm. Learn to do business there.

In I John 2:17, we read, that this world passeth away. This world, which is the physical realm, the Bible says is passing away.

It does not matter whether something is in the spiritual realm or the physical realm. What matters is, can you relate to it? Can you see it, touch it, or feel it whether with your physical senses or spiritual senses? If you can see or feel with your spiritual senses then it exists irrespective of whether or not your physical senses can relate to it.

With this understanding you can talk like God calling those things that be not as though they were. *"(As it is written, I have made thee a father of many nations,) before him whom he believed, even God, who quickeneth the dead, and calleth those things which be not as though they were"* (Romans 4:17). When God is calling those things that be not as though they were, it does not mean those things do not exist and He is just calling them to come into existence. But actually it means they exist in the spiritual realm. It is only not tangible in the physical realm. It is like electricity and magnetism—you don't see them with the physical senses, but you know they exist. So it is with the things of the spirit.

The Kingdom of God, which is in spiritual realm, is superior to the physical realm. And God has already made everything available to you if you are His child in the spiritual realm. What you now need is the how to, the knowledge and capacity to appropriate them into the physical world.

"According as his divine power hath given unto us all things that pertain unto life and godliness, through the knowledge of him that hath called us to glory and virtue" (2 Peter 1:3). God's divine power has provided everything that pertains to life and godliness. Anything that pertains to your ministry, marriage, family, finances, you just name it; it has already been provided in the spiritual realm.

Now get this very key point: It is your actions, words, attitude, and state in the physical realm that determine your ability to receive from the spiritual realm. This should make you attend to your life, prayers, and everything you do in the physical realm with carefulness.

Chapter Four

How to Receive

Now we come to the main thrust of this book. You know God is a giver. You know you have to receive and not achieve. Now how do you receive? If you have not read the preceding chapters, I will humbly advise you not to jump to this chapter, because a clear understanding of the kingdom principle of receiving and the difference between the two realms should be there to be an effective receiver.

I want to emphasize that everything must be received first before you can have. The Holy Spirit, which is a gift of God, must be received. *"For ye have not received the spirit of bondage again to fear; but ye have received the Spirit of adoption, whereby we cry, Abba, Father"* (Romans 8:15). The Spirit of adoption is received. On the other hand others receive the spirit of bondage. If you are full of fear you have received a spirit of bondage. You may say, no. This is what the Scriptures say; and the Scriptures cannot be broken. What you have received is what you will reveal.

The reason fear is revealed in your life is because you have received the spirit of bondage again to fear. Sonship is revealed when the Spirit of adoption is received. We cry, Abba, Father, because the content we have received is the Spirit of sonship. Your content determines your communication.

"God is a Spirit: and they that worship him must worship him in spirit and in truth" (John 4:24). Since God is Spirit, He functions in the spirit. Anyone who wants to relate or reason with God must do so on the plane of the spirit. The spiritual realm is the realm of cause. And the physical realm is the realm where the effects of the causes are deposited or manifested. Those who do business in the spiritual realm will see the wonders of God. *"They that go down to the sea in ships, that do business in great waters; These see the works of the LORD, and his wonders in the deep"* (Psalm 107:23-24). They that do business in the deep they see the wonders of God. Get deeper with God and you will see His wonders. Wonders are normal in the spiritual realm. It is the lifestyle of that realm.

We are also spirit beings. You are a spirit, you have a soul and you live in a body. *"And the very God of peace sanctify you wholly; and I pray God your whole spirit and soul and body be preserved blameless unto the coming of our Lord Jesus Christ"* (1 Thessalonians 5:23).

Your body is your tent and dwelling. *"For we know that if our earthly house of this tabernacle were dissolved, we have a building of God, an house not made with hands, eternal in the heavens"* (2 Corinthians 5:1).

We are the offspring of God. *"For in him we live, and move, and have our being; as certain also of your own poets have said, For we are also his offspring"* (Acts 17:28).

If God is a Spirit and you are His offspring, then you must be a spirit being too. God is also termed the father of spirits. *"Furthermore we have had fathers of our flesh which corrected us, and we gave them reverence: shall we not much rather be in subjection unto the Father of spirits, and live?"* (Hebrews 12:9).

God, being the Father of spirits, means He is the source and sustainer of spirits. It means He is the provider and protector of spirits. He has absolute authority over all spirits. To be spiritually dead means you are separated from the Source and Sustainer of your spirit. So whether you are born again or not, God is the source of your spirit.

With your body you make contact with the physical world and with your spirit you make contact with the spiritual world. God gave you a body to contain Him and a spirit to contact Him. Since we are spirit beings it makes a lot of sense when the Scriptures tell us to live in the Spirit and walk in the Spirit. *"This I say then, Walk in the Spirit, and ye shall not fulfil the lust of the flesh... If we live in the Spirit, let us also walk in the Spirit"* (Galatians 5:16, 25).

The spirit realm is meant to be our natural estate. Adam, before the fall in the Garden, had the ability to live and see in both realms at that same time. Mankind lost that after the fall. In Genesis 3:7, we read, *"And the eyes of them both were opened, and they knew that they were naked; and they sewed fig leaves together, and made themselves aprons."* When the Scripture says their eyes were opened, it means their eyes were awakened to the physical realm more. This is because when man fell the light of his spirit, which was his garment prior to the fall was lost, so now all he could see more and clearly was his physical nakedness and depravity.

Receiving or reception is done or occurs in the spiritual realm. What you do not receive in the spirit, you will never have in the physical realm. But once you lay a hold of it in the spiritual realm you will certainly have a proof in the physical if you don't relinquish your hold. Now you know you receive in the spiritual realm, but how do you receive it? Don't miss out now, because I intend to show you from first principles how you will know when you have received.

Any time the Bible admonishes us to receive, there is another very important word which goes with it. That word is Believe. *"Therefore I say unto you, What things soever ye desire, when ye pray,* **believe** *that ye receive them, and ye shall have them"* (Mark 11:24).

Believe you have received. *"But as many as received him, to them gave he power to become the sons of God, even to them that* **believe** *on his name"* (John1:12).

"But this spake he of the Spirit, which they that **believe** *on him should receive: for the Holy Ghost was not yet given; because that Jesus was not yet glorified"* (John 7:39).

The above Scriptures prove the relationship between believe and receive.

How do I believe I have received?

"Be careful for nothing; but in every thing by prayer and supplication with thanksgiving let your requests be made known unto God" (Philippians 4:6).

"Always in every prayer of mine for you all making request with joy" (Philippians 1:4).

From the two Scriptures above, Paul is saying he

makes requests with joy and thanksgiving. Joy is an emotion—a feeling of excitement. Joy is to experience great pleasure or delight. Joy also means the emotion evoked by well-being, success, or good fortune, or by the prospect of possessing what one desires. At the moment of your request you must be joyful and full of gratitude.

How can I be filled with joy and gratitude when I am still asking or making request? The only way is to assume the feeling that will be yours were you to possess the answer of your request now. You should arouse in you the joy of your desire granted or fulfilled. Contemplate the joy that will be yours were your request an answered prayer, so that you live and move and have your being in the feeling that your desire is fulfilled or your prayer is answered.

If you are able to arrive at this state of joy and continue in it, your answer will manifest with speed in the physical realm. All you have to do is to assume the feeling of joy that would be yours were you already in possession of your request. This is what it means to request with joy. Luke 8:13 says, *"...receiveth with joy."* So you receive with joy. Talk with joy, act with joy, and conduct yourself with joy just as you would if you were already in possession of your request. All the dance you will dance when you have your request in the physical realm, dance it now. The shoutings and the celebrations and the excited state you will display when you have your request, experience them now, whilst you are making your request. Set the moments of joy before you. Psalm 2:11, says, *"...rejoice with trembling."* The rejoicing must be active. You must put all of your heart into it.

This was how Jesus lived.

"Looking unto Jesus the author and finisher of our faith; who for the joy that was set before him endured the cross, despising the shame, and is set down at the right hand of the throne of God" (Hebrews 12:2). Who for the joy that was set before Him. Jesus obtained or received by setting before Him the joy that will be His at the end of His course. He contemplated on it. He placed it before His view. He presented it to His mind. He relished and joyed in the end which He sought. Because He saw it so clearly and felt that joy so well, in the midst of His pain He could whisper to His Father, *"Forgive them for they know not what they do."*

That joy was His strength in His journey. *"For the joy of the Lord is my strength"* (Nehemiah 8:10). Irrespective of your outward circumstances and how you feel you must rejoice. Habakkuk said, *"Although the fig tree shall not blossom, neither shall fruit be in the vines; the labour of the olive shall fail, and the fields shall yield no meat; the flock shall be cut off from the fold, and there shall be no herd in the stalls yet I will rejoice in the LORD, I will joy in the God of my salvation"* (Habakkuk 3:17).

Paul says in Philippians 4:4, *"Rejoice in the Lord always: and again I say, Rejoice."* He also says in I Thessalonians 5:16 to *"Rejoice evermore."* What is Paul saying? Don't rejoice once or twice, but rejoice always. Keep rejoicing. Celebrate the joy. In Psalm 119:162, David says rejoice as one that findeth a great spoil. Rejoice like one who has gotten your answer. Rejoice like one who has gotten his heart's desires already, because in the spirit you have received it. Jump, dance, gyrate, and spin around.

Now, how does joy help?

First, **joy empowers the angels** who deliver your answers.

Second, **joy connects you to Heaven and the throne of God.** *"Thou wilt shew me the path of life: in thy presence is fulness of joy; at thy right hand there are pleasures for evermore"* (Psalm 16:11). Once you are connected to the throne of God, there is a free flow of heavenly resources to you. Hebrews 4:16 says, *"Let us therefore come boldly unto the throne of grace, that we may obtain mercy, and find grace to help in time of need."* Grace is simply the inestimable and inexhaustible riches of Christ in expression. The throne of grace is the royal office that dispenses and distributes the unsearchable riches of Christ. Your connection to that throne brings you into the haven of unlimited heavenly resources. It is joy that connects you to that resource.

Third, **joy brings fruitfulness and abundance**. In Psalm 67:5-6, the psalmist shows us that it is after you have rejoiced and praised God that your ground will yield her increase. (See also Deuteronomy 8:47).

You have to serve God with joyfulness and gladness of heart to see abundance come to you. Abundance and fruitfulness cannot be in view when joy is extinguished. In Joel 1:12, we see when joy withered away from the sons of men, the vine dried up, and the fig tree languished; the pomegranate tree, the palm tree also, and the apple tree, even all the trees of the field, got withered. Beloved when your joy flourishes, your harvest and your desire flourishes.

Now, the question is, how can you feel the joy you will have when your request is granted in the present, at the time of your request? Here is the key: The only way is to see, hear, feel, touch, and smell your request or your desire with your spiritual senses. Below is a paraphrase of 2 Corinthians 4:18, which gives us an overview of what it means to experience joy as though our request has already been granted: *While we look not at the things which are seen, because they are subject to change; but we look at the things unseen, because they are permanent.*

When you are able to see your answer in that realm you now act and talk like God 'who calleth those things that be not as though they were.' Set your mind on things above. Set your mind on things in the spiritual realm. What are the things in the spiritual realm? The very things you are requesting. Seeing with your spiritual eyes is key in this spiritual adventure. You have to see it till you are persuaded and convicted. This is called faith. Seeing the supply of what God has given is the foundation of faith and answered prayer.

Your feelings or emotions are like your hands with which you receive in the spirit. And as you continue in that feeling of joy it will show up in the physical realm. You received it first in the spiritual realm and later it showed up in the physical. With your understanding that the physical realm is a venue, once you receive anything in the spiritual realm you just transport it to the new location— the physical realm. How do you transport it to the physical realm? By your words and actions produced by your joy.

The proof that you have received something in the spiritual realm is seen in your words and your actions. That is how your proof of faith is seen (see Matthew 8:10). Jesus said He never found such great faith. How did He find it? Through the words of the centurion. Faith is a spiritual substance. But how did Jesus see it? He saw it through the words of the centurion. In the same way, Jesus referred to the faith of the woman with the issue of blood. Her faith was seen in her actions. That is how your proof of faith is seen.

The amount of time it takes for what you have received in the spirit to appear in the physical depends on the intensity of your desire and the constancy and consistency with which you continue in the feelings of joy produced by setting your eyes on the answer given to you by God in the spirit. You have to sustain your feelings of joy and your vision or imagination. Don't lose sight of what you have received. Hold on to it unwaveringly.

In I Thessalonians 5:17, you are told to *pray without ceasing*. And in Luke 18:1, Jesus teaches a lesson on persistency. The purpose of persistency in prayer most of the time is to clear your fears, dissolve your doubts, and build faith. The seasons of persistence and importunity produce strong faith and dissolves all doubts. You don't receive only by faith, but the Bible says in Hebrews 6:12 that you inherit what has been promised by faith and patience. The patience is the staying power to hold on to your vision and the feelings of joy irrespective of what happens. You endure by seeing (Hebrews 11:27b). Moses endured by seeing who was invisible. You also endure the invisible realm by seeing. You must see clearly your car, your ministry, your baby, or your marriage in the realm of the spirit. What you see must be more real to you than your circumstances.

We live in a microwave generation where we want everything yesterday. But you will have to learn to hold on to what you have received in the spirit knowing it will certainly arrive in the physical realm.

For example, a relative transfers money to you through Western Union or Money Gram. They only send the control number. Once you get that number, you are excited, you are calm, you start promising people gifts. Why? You have already seen the money in your mind's eyes and so you make plans although you are yet to go receive the physical cash. You are calm about everything and dance about. Why? You are sure you have received the money already because you have the evidence. It is the same with receiving in the realm of the spirit. Your joy is your evidence that you have laid hold of what you desire.

Now it is meditation on God's Word which produces the strength to believe and generates the ability to hold on to what you received in the spirit. Meditation on the Word of God produces revelation or spiritual sight. It destroys doubt and unbelief. Meditation is simply turning the Word of God over and over in your heart. Meditation produces faith.

Faith is the essence of prayer. Faith is generated by a composition of thought and emotion. Faith is the composite of what you see with your spiritual eyes or imagination and the thrill of joy that is produced from what you see. You have to get this point clearly. I said faith is a composition of your thought (what you see in the realm of the spirit through imagination) and joy, which is produced by what you see. With this knowledge you can generate faith any time for anything. And when you have faith you will know you got faith.

So faith is produced when imagination or spiritual sight in the thought realm locks with joy or feeling or emotion. When your thought is fixed on one thing and your emotion is set on the same thing with no wavering or doubt, faith is produced. Once faith is produced, you will certainly see your desire in the physical realm.

Hebrews 11:1 states that faith is the substance of things hoped for, the evidence of things not seen. Faith is both evidence and substance. Things hoped for and things not seen are in the spiritual, invisible realm.

Faith is taking hope, which is a reserve in the spiritual realm and bringing it into the present now. What you hope for has already been reserved for you. By faith you grasp the realities of hope and make it your present day possession. It is the substantiation or solidification of hope. Faith is the lifestyle of the spiritual realm. Faith is the currency of the spiritual realm.

Again, faith is a conviction. Faith is a persuasion. (Romans 4:15) You are persuaded though normal reason of the physical senses will be telling you otherwise. But once you are persuaded of what you have received in the spiritual realm you will not bow to the evidence of facts. But you will stick with the truth.

While we look not at the things which are seen, but we look at the unseen. Now something can be true to your experience and yet not the truth. We see in 2 Corinthians 4:17 that your experience, which is in the seen realm is temporary, that is, subject to change. It does not last. What you see in the physical realm does not mold or shape your life, but rather what you don't see, which is in the unseen realm.

That is why we need our spiritual senses to be awakened so we can see, hear, touch, feel, smell, what God is saying, which is the real thing, the eternal and the truth. At times when you are walking in faith people tell you you must be realistic. What people don't understand is that people of faith are also realists. They just have their foundations in a superior reality. Faith sees in the spiritual realm. It focuses on its purpose. Faith grabs the reality of the spiritual realm and violently brings it into a collision with the physical realm. For the violent taketh it by force (Matthew 11:12).

The key to receiving is to see what is provided in the Kingdom. Seek first the Kingdom always and find what has been delivered to you. Now, by Jesus, the veil has been rent; the way to the holiest has been opened. There is no barrier or toll gate. Every toll has been paid by the blood (Hebrews 10:20). You can now see what is yours without any veil covering your vision.

Now confession of the Word helps you to see the unseen realm. This is because words are pictures or mental images. It makes you see what God is saying. You don't confess the Word so that God will give to you, but because God has already given to you, you confess to see it with your spiritual eyes. When the Scriptures say, God calleth those things that be not as though they were, it means He is calling it because it already exists in the spiritual realm.

For example, when you are in your living room, and your son is in his bedroom, you can call your son to come to the living room. That does not mean your son does not exist. He exists, but he is only in a different location. You are only calling him to appear or to manifest in the living room. In the same way, when you call those things that be not as though they were, they already are in the spiritual realm, you are only calling them to appear in the physical realm. Hallelujah. Your miracle already exists. Your healing and your visions already exist. Words are like containers that carry the substance of things you desire. And the substance of the thing you desire is called faith. So words are carriers of your faith.

And once you see it, it will manifest. St. Augustine said, Faith is to believe what you do not see (in the physical realm); the reward of this faith is to see (in the physical realm) what you believe.

Faith is like a potion or chemical, which when mixed with prayer gives one speedy results. In the laboratory of God, faith is a substance with which you can prepare your answer. In Hebrews 4:2, they failed to mix the Word with faith, so it did not profit them. You can mix your prayer with faith to yield profit.

If you give up on your feelings of joy and thanksgiving what happens is that the answer you received in the spirit from GOD you let go. Once you let it go, it is still available in the spirit. And the enemy, who is a thief, comes to steal, kill, and destroy what belongs to you. God has answered you and given you what you requested. But you gave it up and the enemy stole it. I pray for grace for you to hold on and persist in joy. This process of receiving requires discipline and constant practice to perfect it. It is an art. And like every art it must be practiced to perfection.

Chapter Five

Thoughts and Emotions

Spirit beings elicit thoughts, desires, and emotions. You are a spirit being so you elicit them too. They are invisible to the physical eyes, but they are real to the spiritual man. They are tangible. Thoughts are real; they are actual substances in the spirit realm. The thoughts you think are actual things. They are so powerful they make up a man. As a man thinketh so is he (Proverbs 23.7).

If your thoughts make you, then evil thoughts must be changed to lovely thoughts so your life becomes lovely.

In Philippians 4:8, Paul tells us, *"Finally, brethren, whatsoever things are true, whatsoever things are honest, whatsoever things are just, whatsoever things are pure, whatsoever things are lovely, whatsoever things are of good report; if there be any virtue, and if there be any praise, think on these things."*

These are the kinds of thoughts we should think. Such thoughts make angels feel at home with you.

Thoughts attract spirits. Good thoughts attract good spirits and bad thoughts attract bad spirits. When you get to a place where there is hatred and bitterness and anger you can feel that hatred, bitterness, and anger, because such thoughts attract evil spirits and the place becomes infested with them. On the other hand, when you get to a place where lovely thoughts exists, the atmosphere is refreshing and very inviting, because lovely thoughts attract angelic beings.

If you want your home and your church to be full of angels, then think lovely thoughts.

Emotions are like thoughts, they are visible and they have substance in the realm of the spirit. Emotions appear like fire in the realm of the spirit. Jealousy, which is an emotion, appears like fire in the realm of the spirit (Psalm 79:5 states: "How long, Lord? wilt thou be angry for ever? shall thy jealousy burn like fire?"). (See also Song 8:6, NIV). Jealousy is a mighty flame that burns like a blazing fire. Emotions of anger also appear like fire (Psalm 89:46, NLT, states: "O Lord, how long will this go on? Will you hide yourself forever? How long will your anger burn like fire?"). The aftermath of anger is like smoke (Psalm 74:1 says, "O God, why have you rejected us so long? Why is your anger so intense against the sheep of your own pasture?").

Emotions provide conducive environments for an evil spirit (Colossians 3:2). Emotions animate thoughts; that is to say, it gives life to thought and it makes thought more forceful. What air is to mankind, emotion is to thought. Divine life and energy are released as we set our thoughts and emotions above for every good and perfect gift is from above. Emotions and thoughts of fear, sadness, and depression stifles and steals your miracle, answer, and testimony. And all these are products of unbelief. Emotions of joy, thanksgiving, and love release miracles and answers speedily, and such emotions are products of faith.

Love, praise, and gratitude are the supreme emotions.

Love is a potent force which casts out the spirit called fear. *"There is no fear in love; but perfect love casteth out fear: because fear hath torment. He that feareth is not made perfect in love"* (1 John 4:18). There is no fear in love. When love is present fear runs away and faith comes. Evil forces cannot stand against the love of God. Now faith and fear are arch enemies. Where one is found, the other cannot exist. When faith arrives, fear checks out, and when faith leaves fear reign.

It is love which energises your faith. *"For in Jesus Christ neither circumcision availeth any thing, nor uncircumcision; but faith which worketh by love"* (Galatians 5:6). Faith, which operates by love, is the platform for the production of effective and excellent results in Christ. Your faith will deflate in the absence of love. Desire to walk in love.

"For God hath not given us the spirit of fear; but of power, and of love, and of a sound mind" (2 Timothy 1:7).

God has given you a spirit of love. You don't lack it. Just walk in it.

Don't walk in fear. Fear is a bondage. It is called the spirit of bondage. It causes a man to fear (Romans 8:15).

"Forasmuch then as the children are partakers of flesh and blood, he also himself likewise took part of the same;

that through death he might destroy him that had the power of death, that is, the devil; And deliver them who through fear of death were all their lifetime subject to bondage" (Hebrews 2:14-15).

Fear makes you a slave and servant to the devil and his works. Fear is the easiest conduit to captivity. Fear is an invitation to the devil. Humanity has been held in captivity all these years because of the fear of death. When a man gains mastery over fear, his dominion in life is assured. The first emotion that entered the fallen race was fear. In Genesis 3:10, the man God made was possessed by fear. When he heard the voice of God he became afraid. Now he was in bondage to the wicked taskmaster, the devil. The strong weapon and snare the devil possesses is fear. Once you become afraid the devil launches his attack against you. Fear paralyzes men from advancing into their glorious destinies. Every shackle of fear over your life I command it to be broken in Jesus' mighty name.

A pure heart of love is a great asset. In life, you progress by love, service, and helping others. Selfishness and self interest are hindrances to both spiritual and physical growth.

Praise and thanksgiving are the highest expressions of the faith life or the spiritual life. The life of God within you as a believer is expressed by way of joy. Joy is the echo of God's life and ability in you, and joy is expressed by way of praise. Praise is the expression of overflowing joy. *"In every thing give thanks: for this is the will of God in Christ Jesus concerning you"* (1 Thessalonians 5:18). Thanksgiving is the will of God. It means it is the wisdom of God for your life. And when you forsake the wisdom of

God for your life, the Scriptures say you wrong your own soul (Proverbs 8:36).

It is not just enough for you to receive Christ Jesus; abound in Him with thanksgiving.

"As ye have therefore received Christ Jesus the Lord, so walk ye in him: Rooted and built up in him, and stablished in the faith, as ye have been taught, abounding therein with thanksgiving" (Colossians 2: 6-7).

It is not just enough to pray, but watch in the same with thanksgiving.

"Continue in prayer, and watch in the same with thanksgiving" (Colossians 4:2). Thanksgiving is a demonstration of your faith. Gratitude stabilizes and strengthens the faith of a man. Faith is responding with gratitude to the goodness (provision) of God in Christ. Once the spirit of God spoke in my spirit, faith is thanking God for what HE has already provided.

Thanksgiving provokes supernatural manifestations and triggers divine intervention. Friend, make thanksgiving your lifestyle. Strange miracles and testimonies are your portion as you engage in thanksgiving. Jesus wrought two great miracles through the power of thanksgiving. Jesus thanked God, and two fish and five loaves of bread were multiplied so much so that five thousand men were fed, not counting women and children. Let every good thing in your life be multiplied as you thank God daily. The Scriptures say, God daily loads us with benefits. I believe the loading of those benefits comes through thanksgiving.

Again at the tomb of Lazarus, Jesus again gave thanks and Lazarus came out. Every dead situation resurrects as you give thanks daily in your life.

To complain and to murmur is very evil. Murmuring and complaining are signs of ingratitude. Ingratitude was actually the original sin. (Genesis 3:5). Man was not satisfied being what God had made him. They (Adam and Eve) believed the lie of the devil. They said we want to become something else. Their act told God in the face that what He did was not enough. They wanted more. But it was all based on unbelief in the Word of God, because God had already made them in the best state possible.

Complaining and murmuring delay and hinder the power of God from working in your favour. Do everything without complaining (Philippians 2:14). Nowadays you ask a person, how are you doing and he will respond, "Aah, I can't complain." Men have synthesized new and nice ways to complain. And yet murmuring and complaining is still very detrimental.

When the Israelites murmured as recorded in Numbers 14:11, God asked Moses two questions. First He said, how long will these provoke me? Again God asked, How long will they refuse to believe in me? When you murmur you are making a statement telling God you don't trust Him. When you complain you provoke God. You treat God with contempt when you complain and murmur. To murmur is to reject your place of divine allotment. And when you reject your place of divine allotment, you are exposed to Satan and his agents.

So murmuring and complaining empowers demons and satanic agents to rejoice and steal your answers.

One can so fill himself with love and gratitude and praise for what he has that he does not behold any lack.

And when you don't behold any lack abundance is in view, and what you behold you get. God wanted Abraham to have innumerable descendants so God caused Abraham to behold innumerable stars. When Abraham saw the innumerable stars, he gave glory to God. And in due time his abundance manifested. So abundance begins to flow your way. As you walk in love and gratitude, worry and anxiety leaves automatically.

Anxiety is a tell-tale sign that points to the presence of fear and doubt. Paul says be anxious for nothing, but by prayer and thanksgiving let your request be made known. Thanksgiving and joy destroy anxiety.

To worry is to doubt. And to doubt is to be double minded. James says, *"A double minded man is unstable in all his ways"* (James 1:8).

If you are as unstable as the waters you shall not excel. In Genesis 49:4b, we see Reuben was the excellency of power and dignity of Iis father, Jacob, but because he was unstable, he could not excel. Your glorious and victorious life in Christ can elude you if you become unstable through doubt and worry.

Excellence eludes any person who is unstable in all his ways.

Most people come to God after they have tried all other options and all other options have failed. By the time they come, they are already full of fear and doubt. That is why most of the time God will have to allay your fears and dissolve your doubts by giving you a word of encouragement. God gives encouraging words like, 'I am with you,' 'Do not be afraid.' The Scriptures admonish us several times not to be afraid.

There was a woman who exhibited great faith in the days of Elisha. As recorded in 2 Kings 4:26, her son died and she was in grieve. When she met the prophet before she could make her request or complain or speak of her predicament, she said, "It is well." Hallelujah. What great faith! Like David, she encouraged herself in the Lord.

Chapter Six

The Hindrances to Receiving

The greatest hindrance to receiving from God is not the devil. It is your mind. Are you surprised? Well, let me show you? The devil only takes advantage of your mind to hinder you.

2 Corinthians 10:3-5 states: *"For though we walk in the flesh, we do not war after the flesh: (For the weapons of our warfare are not carnal, but mighty through God to the pulling down of strong holds;) Casting down imaginations, and every high thing that exalteth itself against the knowledge of God, and bringing into captivity every thought to the obedience of Christ"* (KJV).

Paul in his writings reveals the two realms: the flesh realm (physical realm) and the spirit realm. He then goes on to tell us though we walk in the flesh realm or the physical realm, we should not war or do business in the physical realm. We should wage war in the spirit.

Our war in the spirit is to pull down strongholds and to cast down imaginations and every high thing that exalts itself or rears up its head above the knowledge of God. A mental stronghold is a pattern of thoughts which are deep seated. Such thoughts have been strengthened by the emotions. Normally strongholds of the mind are produced by a false reasoning over a long period of time. The 'high thing' refers to a barrier that has been erected in the mind. The knowledge of God is His Word.

What hinders your receiving from God is that thought of doubt and that thought of unbelief that tells you, you cannot have what you have received in the spirit. What the devil does is to play games on your mind. He sends you pictures of defeat, failure, and or disappointment.

For example, if you are not well and lying in the hospital waiting to see the manifestation of your healing, he begins to show you pictures and images of your funeral. He turns your mind into a cinema and shows you how you died in the hospital, and they came for your body, and how a lot of people showed up at your funeral.

But this is the time to take captive and arrest that thought or imagination. That thought or imagination is exalting itself against the knowledge of God, which says, By His stripes you were healed. You've got to arrest that thought.

You arrest the thought by refuting it in the name of Jesus. Many times you refute it once, and it still stays. Maybe the thought still stayed because you were too gentle in refuting it. You have got to shout at the thought. You will have to refute it violently in the name of Jesus. You are undertaking a demolishing exercise. You smash the thought and tear down every barrier erected in the mind in the name of Jesus.

The evil thought came in for a fight. It came into your mind to stand against the knowledge of God. You must also put up a fight. Being gentle on that devilish thought will not change it. The Bible says, *"Resist the devil."* There is no gentleness in resisting. You have to be solid and steadfast in your resistance. That thought came to resist you. The devil is the adversary. He is the opposer. You must resist the opposition steadfastly. Withstand that thought.

Now after arresting the thought, you have to bring it or lead it to the obedience or the submission of Christ. How do you do that? Declare what the Word of God has said concerning your case. Bring that thought to obedience of Christ. The obedience of Christ is the authority of Christ. Lead your thoughts to submit to the authority of Christ by aligning your mind with the Word of God. There is nothing more powerful than the Word of God. When you continue to declare the Word of God, you build enough faith that is stronger than the stronghold in the mind that is hindering you from receiving what you desire of the Lord.

If you don't arrest and bring the thought to the obedience of Christ, and you allow it to linger in your mind long enough, it becomes a stronghold. It becomes a force field that will begin to attract evil circumstances into your life.

To have perpetual victory in the course of your life, you have to renew your mind with the Word of God.

Romans 12:2 tells us: *"And be not conformed to this world: but be ye transformed by the renewing of your mind, that ye may prove what is that good and acceptable, and perfect, will of God"* (KJV).

Your transformation in life only comes by the renewal of your mind. To see your marriage transformed or your finances or any aspect of your life transformed, you must renew your mind. Do you want to see changes in your life, then renew your mind. Change the mindset. Mindset means the mind has been set to a particular frequency like a radio. To renew, change the settings on your mind. You change the settings of your mind with the Word of God.

To renew your mind also means to renovate your mind. It connotes the renovation of a building. Your mind is like a building. You have to build it with the Word of God into a strong and high tower. You have to build bulwarks around it to protect it from the attacks of the adversary, so that when evil thoughts that are not consistent with the Word of God come against you, they bounce off. Build your mind into a stronghold of the knowledge of God.

Second Corinthians 10:5, MSG, says to us: we use our powerful God-tools for smashing warped philosophies, tearing down barriers erected against the truth of God, fitting every loose thought and emotion and impulse into the structure of life shaped by Christ (from THE MESSAGE: The Bible in Contemporary Language © 2002 by Eugene H. Peterson. All rights reserved.)

The Scripture does not only refer to loose thoughts that exalt themselves against the knowledge of God. It refers also to emotions that exalt themselves against the knowledge of God. It is not only thoughts you have to refute and arrest. Emotions of fear, depression, heaviness, anxiety, sorrow, sadness, and envy exalt themselves against the knowledge of God—arrest them and bring them into the obedience of Christ. Inject yourself with emotions of joy, love, and gratitude through meditation on the Word of God and His promises to you.

It was thoughts of doubt and emotions of fear that cut short the fame of Peter walking about 100 meters on water (Matthew 14:23-31). Peter was comfortable walking on water as long as he had his eyes on Christ. His eyes on Christ produced thoughts and emotions of faith and confidence and he walked above the storms of the sea. But everything changed when he took his eyes off Jesus. In verse 30, he saw the boisterous waves, and I believe thoughts of fear came to him. I am sure Peter imagined himself buried under the sea and some fish using his eyes for dinner. Thoughts and images of his funeral went through his mind. As a result thoughts of doubt and emotions of fear inrushed him and he started sinking. There was no time for Peter to arrest those thoughts and emotions. But thank God, Jesus was right there to catch him. I pray that before you sink in life, Jesus, by His act of mercy, will catch you.

In verse 31, Jesus told Peter that the reason for his sinking was his thoughts of doubts. Matthew 14:31: *"And immediately Jesus stretched forth his hand, and caught him, and said unto him, O thou of little faith, wherefore didst thou doubt?"*

Can it be that the reason you are sinking in your marriage, ministry, finances, business, education, or any aspect of your life is simply because thoughts and images from the enemy are passing through your mind? Change your thoughts. Change your emotions. And you will rise above the storms in your life.

To be above the storms of life perpetually, you got to shut out thoughts and emotions of fear by filling your mind with the Word of God (Matthew 14:23-31).

www.ingramcontent.com/pod-product-compliance
Lightning Source LLC
LaVergne TN
LVHW051157080426
835508LV00021B/2670